POWDERED
Bocha Sweet

ALL-PURPOSE
IN THE
RAW®
OPTIMAL
ZERO CALORIE
SWEETENER BLEND

LILY'S
LESS SUGAR · SWEET LIFE™
White Chocolate Style
BAKING CHIPS
Stevia Sweetened

NET WEIGHT 7 OZ (198g)

GOOD DAY™
Rainbow Sprinkles

NET WT. 3 OZ. (85g)

HERSHEY'S
SYRUP

ALL
PLA
ZERO CAL
& ZERO SU

I Don't Eat Sugar!

But I LOVE Sweets! Baker's Buddy

Hello there and WELCOME to Sweet Options Delights! We have compiled these recipes for you as we move away from using white cane sugar in baking. And to ease you into the transition, our recipes are designed for smaller, mini versions of the most delicious cakes and pies! These alternative sweeteners work just as well and we are happy to present them to you!

Not ready to make the switch? No problem! Our recipes can be swapped out for traditional baking ingredients with a 1:1 ratio but we hope you will give the other alternatives a try!

Here is a small list of the sweeteners that we use in our recipes, which can be found in most grocery stores, major food chains and online:

Lakanto(R) Monkfruit Sweetened Maple Flavored Syrup
Purecane(TM) Brown Sweetener
Purecane (TM) Confectioner's Sweetener
Purecane(TM) Granular Baking Sweetener
DateLady (TM) Date Sugar
Carrington Farms(R) BeetRoot Powder
Lily's(R) Baking Chips
Miss Jones Baking Co. Bettersweet(R) Sugar Replacement
Good Dee's(R) Rainbow Sprinkles No Sugar Added
Organic Pyure(TM) Powdered Sweetener - Stevia Blend

There are some Quick Tips included with some of the recipes so be sure to check them out!

Happy Baking!

From S. A. Pierce and the Sweet Options Delights Bakers

BONUS SECTION! We've also included some Yogurt Parfait Ideas that are so tasty! We hope that you will give them a try!

Table of Contents

Cakes and More Treats! 11
Cupcakes! 35
BONUS! Yogurt Parfait Ideas! 51
Index of Recipes 77

Cakes and More Treats!

Walnut and Cinnamon Blondies!

Chopped walnuts mixed into a blonde
cinnamon brownie!

Dry Ingredients
¾ cup of Almond Flour
¼ cup Cassava Flour
1 cup of Brown Granulated Sweetener
A pinch of Salt
1-1/2 teaspoons of Baking Powder
½ teaspoon of Baking Soda
1 teaspoon of Cinnamon
½ cup of chopped Walnuts

Wet Ingredients
2 sticks (1 cup) of Butter
1 whole Egg (at room temp)
1 Egg Yoke

Preheat oven to 350 degrees and have an 8x8 inch square cake pan ready.

Place the butter and brown granulated sweetener in a pan over low heat and stir until the sweetener has dissolved. Cook stirring for an additional minute but do not let mixture boil. Let cool for at least 10 mins.

Stir in the whole egg and egg yoke into the mixture. Add Dry Ingredients and stir until just blended, including the walnuts. Pour the brownie batter into the prepared pan, then bake in the preheated oven for 25-30 mins. or until center is springy.

Once brownies have cooled, use a very sharp knife when ready to cut.

Number of Servings: 6 squares

Prep Time: 30 mins

No-Bake Chocolate Peanut Butter Pie!

Pecan Crust with Cream cheese filling
  and Chocolate Drizzle with mini
  Sugar Free Peanut Butter Cups on
  top!

Pecan Crust
1 Cup of Pecan Flour
¼ Cup of Brown Sweetener
¼ Teaspoon of Cinnamon
3 Tablespoons of Melted Unsalted
  Butter
2 tablespoons of Unsweetened Cocoa
  Powder

Filling
3 oz of Cream Cheese (at room temp)
¼ cup of Powdered Sweetener
2 tablespoons of Milk
½ cup of smooth Peanut Butter
2 tablespoons of Granulated
  Sweetener
¼ cup of cold Whipping Cream

Mix Pecan Crust ingredients in a bowl and spread on the bottom and sides of a 7-inch pie/tart pan.

In a large bowl, mix the cream cheese, powdered sweetener and milk until well blended. Add the peanut butter and mix well.

In a small bowl, add 2 Tbls of granulated sweetener to the Whipping Cream and beat until peaks form. Fold in the whipped cream to the cream cheese mixture until well incorporated. Pour the filling into the pie/tart crust. Smooth the top of the pie and garnish with sugar free peanut butter cups and sugar free chocolate drizzle on top.

Cover and refrigerate for at least 2-3 hours before serving.

Use a very sharp knife when ready to cut!

Number of Servings: 5 to 12 slices

Prep Time: 20 mins

Delicious Coffee Cake Squares!

Yellow cake with cinnamon filling!

Dry Ingredients
1 cup of Almond Flour
½ Cup of Cassava Flour
½ cup of Granulated Sweetener
¼ teaspoon of Salt
1-1/2 teaspoons of Baking Powder
½ teaspoon of Baking Soda

Wet Ingredients
½ cup of Milk
1 Egg
1 teaspoon of Vanilla Extract
½ cup of Oil

Cinnamon Filling
1 tablespoon of Butter (melted)
1 teaspoon of Cinnamon
¼ cup of Brown granulated Sweetener

Preheat oven to 350 degrees and have an 8x8-inch baking dish ready.

In a large bowl, whisk together the oil, milk, sweetener, whole egg and vanilla. Add the flour, baking powder, baking soda and salt to the bowl and mix.

Pour half of the batter into the baking dish.

In a small bowl, combine the Brown granulated Sweetener and Cinnamon and sprinkle over the batter. Drizzle the melted butter over the top and pour the remaining batter over the cinnamon filling.

Cover the dish loosely with foil and bake for 25 mins. Remove the foil and bake 10 mins. or more or until a toothpick comes out clean.

Use a very sharp knife when ready to cut into 9 squares.

Number of Servings: 9 squares

Prep Time: 30 mins

No-Bake Pecan Cheesecake with Maple Glaze!

Pecan Crust
1 Cup of Pecan Flour
¼ Teaspoon of Cinnamon
2 to 3 Tbls of Melted Unsalted Butter

Filling
4 oz of Cream Cheese (at room temp)
¼ cup of Powdered Sweetener Alternative
1 tablespoon of Milk
1 Tsp of Maple Extract
2 tablespoons of Brown granulated Sweetener
¼ cup of cold Whipping Cream
1/3 cup of chopped pecans

Maple Glaze
½ Cup of Brown granulated Sweetener
1 Tablespoon of Sugar Free Maple Syrup
½ Teaspoon Maple Extract
2 Tablespoons of Unsalted Butter (melted)

Mix Pecan Crust ingredients in a bowl and spread on the bottom of a small spring form pan or a small pie tart. (7 inches or less)

In a large bowl, mix the cream cheese, powdered sweetener, maple extract and milk until well blended.

In a small bowl, add 2 Tbls of Brown granulated sweetener to the Whipping Cream and beat until peaks form. Fold in the whipped cream to the cream cheese mixture and add the chopped pecans until well incorporated. Pour the filling into the spring form pan.

Prepare the maple glaze by melting the brown granulated sweetener and butter. Remove from heat then add maple syrup and maple extract. Once cooled, drizzle on top of cheesecake. Smooth the top and garnish with pecan halves.
Cover and refrigerate for at least 3 hours before serving.

Use a very sharp knife when ready to cut.

Number of Servings: 5 to 12 slices

Prep Time: 30 mins

Luscious Banana Buttermilk Cake with Pecans!

Yellow cake, mix mashed bananas in cake mix with Cream cheese frosting and pecans!

Dry Ingredients
1-1/4 cups of Almond Flour
¼ cup Cassava Flour
½ cup of Granulated Sweetener
¼ teaspoon of Salt
1-1/2 teaspoons of Baking Powder
½ teaspoon of Baking Soda
½ teaspoon of Cinnamon

Wet Ingredients
¼ cup of Shortening (palm fruit oil)
½ cup of mashed ripe Bananas
½ cup of Buttermilk
1 Egg (at room temp)

Cream Cheese and Nut Frosting
6 oz of Cream Cheese
5 oz of Unsalted Butter (softened)
2/3 cup of Powdered Sweetener
1-1/2 teaspoons of Vanilla Extract
½ cup of chopped pecans

Preheat oven to 350 degrees and have a 6-inch spring form pan

ready.

In a large bowl, mix the Dry Ingredients together and set aside. In a separate bowl, beat the egg and buttermilk together and then add the Wet Ingredients to the Dry Ingredients bowl. Add the shortening and beat well. Stir in the mashed ripe bananas until well blended.

Place the spring form pan in the oven and bake for 45-50 mins.

For the Cream Cheese and Nut Frosting: In a small bowl, combine the cream cheese and vanilla extract together and the unsalted butter and mix well. Add the Powdered Sweetener to desired consistency. Fold in the chopped pecans.

Once cake has cooled, remove from spring form pan cut in half horizontally. Spread Cream Cheese Nut frosting between layers and outside of cake.

Use a very sharp knife when ready to cut.

Number of Servings: 5 to 12 slices

Prep Time: 1 hour

Cookies And Cream Cake

Chocolate Cake with crumbled
  chocolate sandwich cookie and
  Cream Cheese Frosting!

Dry Ingredients
¾ cup of Almond Flour
¼ cup Cassava Flour
½ cup of Date Sugar
¼ teaspoon of Salt
¼ cup of Unsweetened Cocoa Powder
1 teaspoon of Baking Powder
½ teaspoon of Baking Soda
1/3 cup of crumbled sugar free
  chocolate sandwich cookies

Wet Ingredients
1 cup of Milk
1 Egg
1 teaspoon of Vanilla Extract
¼ cup of Shortening (palm fruit oil)

Cream Cheese Frosting
4 oz of Cream Cheese
½ cup of Powdered Sweetener
  Alternative
1 teaspoon of Vanilla Extract
½ cup of cold Whipping Cream
1/4 cup of crumbled sugar free
  chocolate sandwich cookies

Preheat oven to 350 degrees and have a 6-inch spring form pan ready.

In a large bowl, mix the Dry Ingredients together. In a separate bowl, mix all Wet Ingredients together and beat until well blended. Add the wet ingredients to the dry ingredients bowl and use a beater to mix well. Fold in 1/3 cup of crumbled sugar free chocolate sandwich cookies.

Place the spring form pan in the oven and bake for 40-45 mins. or until toothpick comes out clean.

For the Cream Cheese Frosting: In a small bowl, combine the cream cheese and vanilla extract together and mix well. Add the Powdered Sugar alternative to desired consistency. In a separate bowl, beat the Whipping Cream until peaks form and blend well with cream cheese mixture. Fold in 1/4 cup of crumbled sugar free chocolate sandwich cookies.

Once cake has cooled, remove from spring form pan cut in half horizontally. Spread Cream Cheese frosting between layers and outside of cake. Decorate with whole sandwich cookies.

Use a very sharp knife when ready to cut!

Number of Servings: 5 to 11 slices

Prep Time: 1 hour

Strawberries and Cream Cake!

Buttery Vanilla Cake with Strawberry
  Cream Cheese frosting!

Dry Ingredients
¾ cup of Almond Flour
¼ cup of Cassava Flour
½ cup of Granulated Sweetener
¼ teaspoon of Salt
1 teaspoon of Baking Powder
½ teaspoon of Baking Soda

Wet Ingredients
¼ cup of Milk
1 Egg
1 teaspoon of Vanilla Extract
¼ cup of Oil
4 tablespoons of Unsalted Butter
  (softened)

Cream Cheese Frosting
4 oz of Cream Cheese
½ cup of Powdered Sweetener
1 teaspoon of Vanilla Extract
¼ cup of cold Whipping Cream
¼ cup of frozen strawberries (thawed
  and pureed)
1 Packet of Stevia Sweetener

Preheat oven to 350 degrees and have a 6-inch spring form pan ready.

Take a handful of thawed strawberries through a food processor until slightly pureed. Add 1 packet of Stevia Sweetener to the fruit.

In a large bowl, mix the Dry Ingredients together. In a separate bowl, mix all Wet Ingredients together and beat until well blended. Add the dry ingredients to the wet ingredients bowl and use a beater to mix well.

Place the spring form pan in the oven and bake for 30-40 mins. or until toothpick comes out clean.

For the Strawberry Cream Cheese Frosting: In a small bowl, combine the cream cheese and vanilla extract together and mix well. Add the Powdered Sweetener to desired consistency. Stir in the strawberry puree. In a separate bowl, beat the Whipping Cream until peaks form and blend well with cream cheese mixture.

Once cake has cooled, remove from spring form pan. Cut horizontally and spread Cream Cheese frosting in between layers and outside of cake.

Use a very sharp knife when ready to cut.

Number of Servings: 5 to 12 slices

Prep Time: 40 mins

Red Velvet Delight!

Red cake using beetroot powder with
  Cream cheese frosting!

Dry Ingredients
¾ cup of Almond Flour
¼ cup of Cassava Flour
½ cup of Granulated Sweetener
A pinch of Salt
1 teaspoon of Baking Powder
3 tablespoons of Beetroot Powder*
1 tbls of Cocoa Powder

Wet Ingredients
¼ cup of Buttermilk
1-1/2 teaspoons of white Vinegar*
¼ cup of Olive Oil
1 Egg
1 teaspoon of Vanilla Extract

Cream Cheese Frosting
4 oz of Cream Cheese
½ cup of Powdered Sweetener
1 teaspoon of Vanilla Extract
½ cup of cold Whipping Cream

Preheat oven to 350 degrees and have a 6-inch spring form pan
ready.

In a large bowl, mix the Dry Ingredients together. In a separate bowl, mix all Wet Ingredients together and beat until well blended. Add the wet ingredients to the Dry Ingredients bowl and use a beater to mix well.

Place the spring form pan in the oven and bake for 40-45 mins. or until toothpick comes out clean.

For the Cream Cheese Frosting: In a small bowl, combine the cream cheese and vanilla extract together and mix well. Add the Powdered Sweetener to desired consistency. In a separate bowl, beat the Whipping Cream until peaks form and blend well with cream cheese.

Once cake has cooled, remove from spring form pan cut in half horizontally. Spread Cream Cheese frosting between layers and outside of cake. Sprinkle cake crumbs on frosting.

Use a very sharp knife when ready to cut.

Number of Servings: 5 to 12 slices

Prep Time: 40 mins

Personal Notes: Quick Tips

When the cake is cooled, shave off the peak top of the cake and crumble up to add on the frosting

* You can add more beetroot powder to make the cake batter more red or use natural food coloring drops

* Adding a small amount of white vinegar gives that little tanginess to the cake and also it reacts with the baking soda for a nice fluffy cake

Carrot Cake Supreme!

Cake mixed with shredded carrot and pineapple with Cream cheese frosting and walnuts on top!

Dry Ingredients
¾ cup of Almond Flour
¼ cup Cassava Flour
½ cup of Brown granulated Sweetener
¼ cup of Granulated Sweetener
¼ teaspoon of Salt
1 small Carrot (shredded)
1 teaspoon of Baking Powder
½ teaspoon of Baking Soda
½ teaspoon of Cinnamon
¼ teaspoon of Nutmeg
½ cup of chopped Walnuts

Wet Ingredients
1/4 Cup of crushed Pineapple
1 Egg
1 teaspoon of Vanilla Extract
¼ cup of Oil

Cream Cheese Frosting
4 oz. of Cream Cheese
½ cup of Powdered Sweetener
1 teaspoon of Vanilla Extract
¼ cup of cold Whipping Cream

Preheat oven to 350 degrees and have a 6-inch spring form pan ready.

In a large bowl, whisk the granulated sweeteners, oil, egg, crushed pineapple and vanilla extract together in a large bowl until combined and no brown sweetener lumps in the mix.

In a separate bowl, whisk the flours, baking powder, baking soda, salt, cinnamon and nutmeg together. Add the wet ingredients to the Dry Ingredients bowl and fold ingredients together until just combined. Fold in the carrots and mix well.

Place the spring form pan in the oven and bake for 40-45 mins. or until toothpick comes out clean.

For the Cream Cheese Frosting: In a small bowl, combine the cream cheese and vanilla extract together and mix well. Add the Powdered Sweetener to desired consistency.

In a separate bowl, beat the Whipping Cream until peaks form and blend well with cream cheese.

Once cake has cooled, remove from spring form pan. Spread Cream Cheese frosting on outside of cake. Sprinkle chopped walnuts on top of frosting.
Use a very sharp knife when ready to cut.

Number of Servings: 5 to 12 slices

Prep Time: 1 hour

Copycat O.G. Lemon Cream Cake!

Yellow cake with Lemon Cream Cheese filling and Crumb topping

Dry Ingredients
1 Cup of Almond Flour
½ Cup of Cassava Flour
½ Cup of Granulated Sweetener
¼ Teaspoon of Salt
1 Teaspoon of Baking Powder
½ Teaspoon of Baking Soda

Wet Ingredients
½ Cup of Milk
1 Egg
½ Teaspoon of Vanilla Extract
1 Teaspoon of Lemon Extract
1 Tablespoon of Lemon Juice
¼ Cup of Oil

Lemon Cream Filling
4 oz of Cream Cheese
½ Cup of Powdered Sweetener
2 Tablespoons of Lemon Juice
½ Cup of Heavy Whipping Cream

Crumb Topping
1/3 Cup of Almond Flour
¼ Cup of Powdered Sweetener
2 Tablespoons of Cold Butter
½ Teaspoon of Vanilla Extract

Preheat oven to 325 degrees and have a 6-inch pan ready.

In a large bowl, mix the flours, salt, baking powder and baking soda. In a separate bowl, mix granulated sweetener and all Wet Ingredients together and beat until well blended. Add the wet ingredients to the Dry Ingredients bowl and mix well.
Pour into 6-inch cake pan and bake for 40-45 mins.

Lemon Cream Filling: Beat the Heavy Whipping Cream until peaks form. Mix together Cream Cheese, Powdered Sweetener and Lemon Juice. Fold in Cream Cheese mixture with the Heavy Whipping Cream until blended.

Crumb Topping: In a small bowl, combine Almond Flour and Powdered Sweetener, add cold Butter and dribble in Vanilla

Extract using a fork (or food processor) to achieve crumb consistency.

Once the cake has cooled, remove from the pan and slice cake in half. Spread Lemon Cream filling in between layers, on top and sides of cake. Then place Crumb Topping on top and on the sides of cake.

Chill cake for 3 hours minimum and tap powdered sweetener on top is optional!

Number of Servings: 5 to 11 slices

Prep Time: 1 hour, 15 mins

Personal Notes: Did you ever enjoy that wonderful Lemon Cream Cake from Olive Garden™ and they took it off the menu? Well we've recreated it here!

Nutty Me Crazy Cake Cheesecake!

Chocolate cake with Peanut Butter Cheesecake filling and Chocolate Glaze!

Dry Ingredients
¾ cup of Almond Flour
¼ cup Cassava Flour
½ cup of Date Sugar
¼ teaspoon of Salt
¼ cup of Unsweetened Cocoa Powder
1 teaspoon of Baking Powder
½ teaspoon of Baking Soda

Wet Ingredients
1 cup of Milk
1 Egg
1 teaspoon of Vanilla Extract
¼ cup of Shortening or Oil

Cheesecake Filling
4 oz of Cream Cheese or Neufchatel (at room temp)
2 tablespoons of Butter (at room temp)
½ cup of Powdered Sweetener
1 teaspoon of Vanilla Extract
¼ cup of Peanut Butter (or any Nut Butter)

Chocolate Glaze *
2 tablespoons of Butter
¼ cup of Powdered Sweetener (adjust as needed)
1 tablespoon of Cocoa
2 tablespoons of Milk

Preheat oven to 325 degrees and have a 6-inch spring form pan ready.

In a large bowl, mix the Dry Ingredients together. In a separate bowl, mix all Wet Ingredients together and beat until well blended. Add the wet ingredients to the Dry Ingredients bowl and use a beater to mix well. Add Shortening or oil in last and set aside.

To save on bowls, wash out the Wet Ingredients bowl and reuse for the next step.

Using a beater, cream the Butter and Cream Cheese together. Add the Peanut Butter and the Vanilla Extract and blend. Add the Powdered Sweetener a little at a time until well incorporated.

Pour the cake batter into the 6-inch spring form pan. Pour the cheesecake batter on top of the cake batter and spread evenly.

Place the spring form pan in the oven and for 30 minutes. When cake is done, DO NOT remove from the oven. Turn the oven off and allow the cake to sit in the oven for another 30 minutes to cool gradually.

*Chocolate Glaze - Mix butter, milk and cocoa. Heat over a low flame but do not boil. Remove from heat and add powdered sweetener a little at a time until desired consistency. Drizzle over cake.

Store in refrigerator for up to 5-7 days. Use a very sharp knife when ready to cut.

Number of Servings: 5 to 12 slices

Prep Time: 1 hour

Personal Notes: Quick Tip - *For the Chocolate Drizzle, you can purchase a Sugar Free Chocolate Syrup which also does the trick!

Cupcakes!

Vanilla Almond Cupcakes!

Yellow Cake with Almond Buttercream Frosting

Dry Ingredients
¾ cup of Almond Flour
¼ cup Cassava Flour
½ cup of Granulated Sweetener
¼ teaspoon of Salt
2 teaspoons of Baking Powder

Wet Ingredients
2/3 cup of Milk
1 whole Egg and 1 Egg Yoke
1 teaspoon of Vanilla Extract
1 teaspoon of Almond Extract
1 stick of Unsalted Butter (at Room Temp)

Buttercream Icing
1 Cup of Powdered Sweetener
2 Tablespoons of Milk
1-1/2 Teaspoons Almond Extract
1 Tbls of Unsalted Butter (at Room Temp)

Preheat oven to 350 degrees and have a 6- or 12-cup muffin pan ready.

In a large bowl, cream the granulated sweetener and unsalted butter together. Add the whole egg, egg yoke, milk and the Almond and Vanilla Extracts until blended.

In a separate bowl, mix the Almond and Cassava flours, baking powder and salt together. Add the dry ingredients to the wet ingredients bowl.

Evenly divide the batter between the muffin cups and bake for 25-30 mins.

While the cupcakes are cooling, blend the powdered sweetener and butter. Add the milk and almond extract until combined.

Spread frosting on cupcakes or use a piping bag to decorate and add sprinkles!

Number of Servings: 6 or 12 Cupcakes

Prep Time: 30 mins

Peanut Butter Overload Cupcakes!

Peanut Butter cake with Peanut Butter frosting and chopped peanuts on top!

Dry Ingredients
1 cup of Almond Flour
½ cup Cassava Flour
¾ cup of Granulated Sweetener
¼ teaspoon of Salt
2 teaspoons of Baking Powder

Wet Ingredients
¾ cup of Milk
1 Egg
1 teaspoon of Vanilla Extract
½ cup of Peanut Butter
½ cup of oil

Peanut Butter Frosting
1/4 cup of Peanut Butter
1 Cup of Powdered Sweetener
2 Tablespoons of Milk
½ Teaspoon Vanilla Extract
1 Tablespoon of Unsalted Butter

Preheat oven to 350 degrees and have a 6- or 12-cup muffin pan ready.

In a large bowl, mix the granulated sweetener and the oil. Add the egg, milk and the Vanilla Extract until blended.

In a separate bowl, mix the Almond flour, cassava flour, baking powder and salt together. Mix the dry ingredients to the wet ingredients bowl. Add in the Peanut Butter.
Evenly divide the batter between the muffin cups and bake for 25-30 mins.

While the cupcakes are cooling, combine all ingredients for Peanut Butter Frosting and mix well.

Spread on cupcakes or use a piping bag to decorate and add extra peanuts!

Number of Servings: 6 or 12 Cupcakes

Prep Time: 30 mins

Personal Notes: You can try any Nut Butter as substitution!

Caramel Apple Cupcakes!

Almond cake with apples and caramel frosting!

All Ingredients
2 eggs
½ cup of Brown granulated sweetener
½ cup of white granulated sweetener
½ cup of oil
2 Tsp of Vanilla Extract
1 cup of Almond Flour
¼ cup of Cassava Flour
2 Tsp of Baking Powder
½ Tsp Cinnamon
¼ Tsp Salt
1 Cup of shredded or diced Granny Smith Apple

Caramel Icing
¼ Cup of Brown granulated Sweetener
¾ Cup of Powdered Sweetener
1 Tablespoon of Milk
½ Teaspoon Vanilla Extract
1 tablespoon of Unsalted Butter
A Pinch of Salt

Preheat oven to 350 degrees and have a 6- or 12-cup muffin pan ready.

In a large bowl, mix the brown granulated sweetener and white granulated sweetener together and the oil. Add in the eggs one at a time until blended. Next, add the Vanilla Extract.

In a separate bowl, mix the Almond flour, cassava flour, baking powder, cinnamon and salt together. Add the dry ingredients to the wet ingredients bowl. Stir in the shredded or diced apples. Evenly divide the batter between the muffin cups and bake for 25-30 mins.

While the cupcakes are cooling, add the Brown granulated sweetener to a small pot and butter. Allow both to melt and add the milk. Remove from heat and add powdered sweetener, vanilla extract and pinch of salt and stir until combined.

Once the icing has cooled, spread on cupcakes or use a piping bag to decorate!

Number of Servings: 6 or 12 Cupcakes

Prep Time: 30 mins

Peach Cobbler Cupcakes!

Vanilla Buttermilk cake with diced
  peaches and Cream cheese frosting!

Dry Ingredients
1 cup of Almond Flour
½ cup of Cassava Flour
¾ cup of Granulated Sweetener
¼ teaspoon of Salt
2 teaspoons of Baking Powder

Wet Ingredients
1 Whole Egg
½ Cup of Buttermilk
1 Teaspoon of Vanilla Extract
¼ Teaspoon of Almond Extract
½ cup of Oil
½ cup of diced peaches (fresh or
  frozen)

Cream Cheese Frosting
4 oz. of Cream Cheese
½ cup of Powdered Sweetener
1 teaspoon of Vanilla Extract
¼ cup of cold Whipping Cream

Preheat oven to 350 degrees and have a 6 or 12- cup muffin pan
ready.

In a large bowl, mix the Dry Ingredients together. In a separate bowl, mix all Wet Ingredients together and beat until well blended. Add the wet ingredients to the dry ingredients bowl and mix well. Fold in ½ cup of diced peaches. Reserve some or slices for decorating.

Place the muffin pan in the oven and bake for 25-30 mins.

For the Cream Cheese Frosting: In a small bowl, combine the cream cheese and vanilla extract together and mix well. Add the Powdered Sweetener to desired consistency. In a separate bowl, beat the Whipping Cream until peaks form and fold into the cream cheese mixture.

Once cupcakes have cooled, spread Cream Cheese frosting on top or use a piping bag. Decorate with remaining peaches.

Number of Servings: 6 or 12 Cupcakes

Prep Time: 30 mins

A Chocoholic's Dream Cupcake!

Chocolate cake, Chocolate Frosting
and Chocolate Chips!

Dry Ingredients
1 cup of Almond Flour
½ cup Cassava Flour
¾ cup of Granulated Sweetener
¼ teaspoon of Salt
¼ cup of Unsweetened Cocoa Powder
2 teaspoons of Baking Powder

Wet Ingredients
¾ cup of Milk
1 Egg
1 teaspoon of Vanilla Extract
½ cup of oil

Chocolate Frosting
1 Tbls of unsweetened Cocoa
1 Cup of Powdered Sweetener
1 Tablespoon of Milk
½ Teaspoon Vanilla Extract
1 Tablespoon of Unsalted Butter

Preheat oven to 350 degrees and have a 6- or 12-cup muffin pan
ready.

In a large bowl, mix the granulated sweetener and the oil. Add the egg, milk and the Vanilla Extract until blended.

In a separate bowl, mix the Almond flour, cassava flour, baking powder and salt together. Add the unsweetened Cocoa Powder. Mix the dry ingredients to the wet ingredients bowl.

Evenly divide the batter between the muffin cups and bake for 25-30 mins.

While the cupcakes are cooling, add the unsweetened cocoa in a small pot and butter. Allow both to melt and add the milk. Remove from heat and add powdered sweetener and vanilla extract until combined.

Once the frosting has cooled, spread on cupcakes or use a piping bag to decorate and add mini Sugar Free chocolate morsels!

Number of Servings: 6 or 12 Cupcakes

Prep Time: 30 mins

Pineapple Hummingbird Cupcakes!

Vanilla cake with pineapple and
banana with Cream cheese frosting
and pecans on top!

Dry Ingredients
1 cup of Almond Flour
½ cup of Cassava Flour
½ cup of Granulated Sweetener
¼ teaspoon of Salt
2 teaspoons of Baking Powder
1 teaspoon of Cinnamon

Wet Ingredients
1 Whole Egg
1 Teaspoon of Vanilla Extract
½ cup of Oil
1 small ripe banana, mashed
1/3 cup of crushed pineapple

Cream Cheese Frosting
4 oz of Cream Cheese
½ cup of Powdered Sweetener
1 teaspoon of Vanilla Extract
¼ cup of cold Whipping Cream

Preheat oven to 325 degrees and have a 6 or 12- cup muffin pan
ready.

In a large bowl, mix the Dry Ingredients together. In a separate bowl, mix all Wet Ingredients together and beat until well blended. Add the wet ingredients to the dry ingredients bowl and mix well. Fold in the pineapple and banana. Reserve some pineapple for decorating.

Place the muffin pan in the oven and bake for 35-40 mins.

For the Cream Cheese Frosting: In a small bowl, combine the cream cheese and vanilla extract together and mix well. Add the Powdered Sweetener to desired consistency.

In a separate bowl, beat the Whipping Cream until peaks form and fold into the cream cheese mixture.

Once cupcakes have cooled, spread Cream Cheese frosting on top or use a piping bag. Decorate with remaining pineapple, pecan halves and pieces.

Number of Servings: 6 or 12 Cupcakes

Prep Time: 30 mins

Blueberry Cream Cupcakes!

Blueberry cupcakes with Blueberry
  Cream cheese frosting!

Dry Ingredients
1 cup of Almond Flour
½ cup of Cassava Flour plus 1
  teaspoon
¾ cup of Granulated Sweetener
¼ teaspoon of Salt
2 teaspoons of Baking Powder

Wet Ingredients
1 Whole Egg
½ Cup of Buttermilk
1 Teaspoon of Vanilla Extract
¼ Teaspoon of Almond Extract
½ cup of Oil
2/3 cup of fresh blueberries (divided)

Cream Cheese Frosting
4 oz of Cream Cheese
½ cup of Powdered Sweetener
1 teaspoon of Vanilla Extract
2 Tbls of Unsalted Butter
1/3 cup of crushed blueberries

Preheat oven to 325 degrees and have a 6 or 12- cup muffin pan
ready.

In a large bowl, mix the Dry Ingredients together. In a separate bowl, mix all Wet Ingredients together and beat until well blended. Take 1/3 cup of the blueberries and smash them with a fork in a bowl. Add the wet ingredients to the dry ingredients bowl and mix well.

Next, take 1 tsp of flour and toss the remaining 1/3 cup of blueberries. Then gently fold into the cake batter. Do not over mix. Reserve some for decorating.

Place the muffin pan in the oven and bake for 35-40 mins.

For the Blueberry Cream Cheese Frosting: Finely crush the blueberries in a food processor or use a rolling pin. In a small bowl, combine the cream cheese and butter together then add the vanilla extract, blueberries and mix well. Add the Powdered Sweetener to desired consistency.

Once cupcakes have cooled, spread the Blueberry Cream Cheese frosting on top or use a piping bag. Decorate with remaining blueberries is optional.

Number of Servings: 6 or 12 Cupcakes

Prep Time: 40 mins

Personal Notes: Quick Tip: Lightly coating any added ingredient with a dusting of flour will keep it suspended in the batter during baking and not sink to the bottom. This works very well with fruit, chips, etc.

BONUS! Yogurt Parfait Ideas!

Pineapple and Mandarin Oranges Parfait!

¼ Cup of Chunk Pineapple

1 Mandarin Orange, sliced

1 Vanilla or Coconut Flavored Yogurt

Granola

Add chunk pineapple and sliced mandarin oranges layered with yogurt and granola!

Number of Servings: 2 to 4 servings

Prep Time: 15 mins

Mango and White Cherries Parfait!

1 Mango chopped

A handful of White Cherries, pitted and halved

Favorite Cereal

Plain or Vanilla Yogurt

Chop the mango and set aside. Prepare the white cherries and layer with the mango, favorite cereal and yogurt and enjoy!

Number of Servings: 2 to 4 servings

Prep Time: 15 mins

Red Grapes and Honey Parfait!

½ Cup of Red Grapes, halved

1 Cup of Honey or Vanilla Yogurt

¼ Tsp of Ground Ginger

½ Cup of Granola

1 Tablespoon of Honey or other Sweetener, drizzled on top

Halve the grapes then mix the ground ginger and sweetener together to sprinkle on top!

Number of Servings: 2 to 4 servings

Prep Time: 15 mins

Citrus Fruits & Poms with Ginger Sugar Parfait!

1 Cup of Plain or Vanilla Yogurt

1 Mandarin Orange, sliced

1 Grapefruit, in chunks

1 Pomegranate (seeds)

With pomegranate seeds, grapefruit chunks and mandarin orange slices, mix 2 packets of Splenda with 1/4 Tsp of ground ginger and sprinkle over grapefruit!

Number of Servings: 2 to 4 servings

Prep Time: 15 mins

Strawberry Shortcake Parfait!

Vanilla Sponge Cake Dessert Cups

Handful of sliced strawberries, coated in Splenda

1 Cup of Vanilla or Strawberry Yogurt

A Dollop of Whipped Cream

Toss the sliced strawberries in a packet of Splenda and allow to sit for 10-15 minutes. Cut sponge cakes into quarters and layer with yogurt and strawberries with whipped cream on top!

Number of Servings: 2 to 4 servings

Prep Time: 15 mins

Apple and Peanut Butter Parfait!

1 Apple cut into bite size pieces

1 Cup of Plain or Vanilla Yogurt

½ Teaspoon of Cinnamon

1 Tablespoon of Honey or other Sweetener

2 Tablespoons of Peanut Butter drizzled on top

Peanuts, granola

Chop apple and layer ingredients then top with peanuts and honey!

Number of Servings: 2 to 4 servings

Prep Time: 15 mins

Apple Pie Parfait!

1 Apple

1 Cup of Plain or Vanilla Yogurt

1 or 2 shakes of Cinnamon and Nutmeg

1 Tablespoon of Honey or other Sweetener

Handful of chopped Walnuts

Favorite Granola

Chop the apple and layer remaining ingredients!

Number of Servings: 2 to 4 servings

Prep Time: 15 mins

Berries and Biscoff(TM) Parfait!

1 pkg of Biscoff cookies crushed

1 Cup of Plain or Vanilla Yogurt

Fresh Strawberries, sliced

Fresh Blueberries

1/3 cup of Granola

A Drizzle of Honey

Slice strawberries and crush cookies, layer throughout with a drizzle of honey on top!

Number of Servings: 2 to 4 servings

Prep Time: 15 mins

Honey Nectarine and Mandarin Oranges Parfait!

Favorite Vanilla Cereal

1 Cup of Peach Yogurt

1 Mandarin Orange, sliced

1 Nectarine, chopped

1 Tablespoon of Honey or other Sweetener

Handful of chopped Cashews

Chop the nectarine and layer ingredients, drizzle honey on top!

Number of Servings: 2 to 4 servings

Prep Time: 15 mins

Pina Colada Parfait!

Pineapple chunks

Coconut and Vanilla Flavored Yogurt

A Sponge Dessert Cake soaked in pineapple juice

Raw or Roasted Coconut flakes

Honey Drizzle

Layer pineapple chunks with yogurt and sponge dessert cakes soaked in pineapple juice. Spread Yogurt and coconut flakes throughout and top with a drizzle of honey!

Number of Servings: 2 servings

Prep Time: 15 mins

Apples and Strawberries Parfait!

1 Apple, chopped

Handful of sliced strawberries

1 Cup of Plain or Vanilla Yogurt

1 Tablespoon of Honey or other Sweetener

Handful of chopped Walnuts

Apple Cinnamon Granola

Chop the apple into bite-sized pieces and slice fresh strawberries. Add the yogurt and layer with granola and walnuts with a drizzle of honey!

Number of Servings: 2 to 4 servings

Prep Time: 15 mins

Banana, Walnut and Chocolate Parfait!

1 Banana, sliced

Banana Flavored Yogurt

Sugar-Free Chocolate chips

Vanilla Cereal

Handful of chopped walnuts

Honey Drizzle

Slice the banana and layer with yogurt, cereal, sugar-free chocolate chips and walnuts. Drizzle honey on top!

Number of Servings: 2 Servings

Prep Time: 10 mins

Apple and Banana Walnut Parfait!

1 Apple cut into bite size pieces

1 Cup of Plain or Vanilla Yogurt

1 Small Banana sliced

½ Teaspoon of Cinnamon

1 Tablespoon of Honey or other Sweetener

1/3 Cup of chopped Walnuts

¼ Cup of Granola (optional)

Chop up the apple and slice the banana. Layer ingredients up to the top!

Number of Servings: 2 to 4 servings

Prep Time: 15 mins

Banana Split Parfait!

1 Banana

1 Cup of Plain or Vanilla Yogurt

Fresh Strawberries, sliced

Pineapple Tidbits

1/4 cup of chopped Walnuts

Cherries on top

Drizzle of Chocolate Syrup

Slice the banana and strawberries, with chopped walnuts and cherries on top!

Number of Servings: 2 to 4 servings

Prep Time: 15 mins

Pineapple, Pear and Plum Parfait!

¼ Cup of Pineapple chunks

1 Pear, chopped

1 Plum, chopped

1 Vanilla Yogurt

1 Cherry Yogurt

Honey Drizzle

Granola

Chop all fruits and layer with yogurt and granola. Top with a drizzle of honey!

Number of Servings: 2 to 4 servings

Prep Time: 15 mins

Apples, Cranberries and Orange Parfait!

1 Apple, chopped

1 Mandarin or Navel Orange, sliced

2 Tbls of chopped Dried Cranberries

Vanilla and Mango Flavored Yogurt

Apple Cinnamon Granola

Honey Drizzle

A handful of chopped walnuts

Chop the apple and slice the orange, layer with yogurt, granola and cranberries. Add walnuts and drizzle honey on top!

Number of Servings: 2 to 4 servings

Prep Time: 15 mins

Pear and Plum Parfait!

Cup of Honey or Vanilla Yogurt

1 Pear, Chopped

1 Plum, Chopped

Granola

Dash of Cinnamon

Honey drizzle

Chopped Pecans

Chop the Pear and Plum in bite-sized pieces and layer with remaining ingredients with a drizzle of honey and a dash of cinnamon on top!

Number of Servings: 2 to 4 servings

Prep Time: 15 mins

Chocolate Strawberries Parfait!

2 Shortbread cookies, 1 crushed, 1 half

1 Cup of Strawberry Yogurt

1 Cup of Chocolate Yogurt

Fresh Strawberries, sliced

Chocolate chips

A Drizzle of Chocolate

For the chocolate yogurt, mix your favorite plain or vanilla yogurt with a swirl of zero sugar chocolate syrup. Slice the fresh strawberries and layer with sugar free chocolate chips and yogurt. Add in the cookies and enjoy!

Number of Servings: 2 to 4 servings

Prep Time: 15 mins

Tropical Fruit Parfait!

1 Banana, sliced

2-3 Tablespoons of Toasted Coconut

Pineapple Tidbits

1 Kiwi, chopped

1 Cup of Coconut or Vanilla Yogurt

¼ Cup of Granola or cereal flakes

1 Tablespoon of Honey or other Sweetener, drizzled on top

Toast the coconut in a pan, no oils needed. Once it begins to brown and fragrant, it is ready. Or have the coconut raw, either way! Slice the banana and kiwi and layer with a drizzle of honey on top!

Number of Servings: 2 to 4 servings

Prep Time: 15 mins

Notes

Notes

Notes

Notes

Index of Recipes

A Chocoholic's Dream Cupcake! - *45*
Apple and Banana Walnut Parfait! - *65*
Apple and Peanut Butter Parfait! - *58*
Apple Pie Parfait! - *59*
Apples and Strawberries Parfait! - *63*
Apples, Cranberries and Orange Parfait! - *68*

Banana Split Parfait! - *66*
Banana, Walnut and Chocolate Parfait! - *64*
Berries and Biscoff(TM) Parfait! - *60*
Blueberry Cream Cupcakes! - *49*

Caramel Apple Cupcakes! - *41*
Carrot Cake Supreme! - *27*
Chocolate Strawberries Parfait! - *70*
Citrus Fruits & Poms with Ginger Sugar Parfait! - *56*
Cookies And Cream Cake - *21*
Copycat O.G. Lemon Cream Cake! - *30*

Delicious Coffee Cake Squares! - *15*

Honey Nectarine and Mandarin Oranges Parfait! - *61*

Luscious Banana Buttermilk Cake with Pecans! - *19*

Mango and White Cherries Parfait! - *54*

No-Bake Chocolate Peanut Butter Pie! - *14*
No-Bake Pecan Cheesecake with Maple Glaze! - *17*
Nutty Me Crazy Cake Cheesecake! - *33*

Peach Cobbler Cupcakes! - *43*
Peanut Butter Overload Cupcakes! - *39*
Pear and Plum Parfait! - *69*
Pina Colada Parfait! - *62*
Pineapple and Mandarin Oranges Parfait! - *53*
Pineapple Hummingbird Cupcakes! - *47*
Pineapple, Pear and Plum Parfait! - *67*

Red Grapes and Honey Parfait! - *55*
Red Velvet Delight! - *25*

Strawberries and Cream Cake! - *23*
Strawberry Shortcake Parfait! - *57*

Tropical Fruit Parfait! - *71*

Vanilla Almond Cupcakes! - *37*

Walnut and Cinnamon Blondies! - *13*

Made in United States
Orlando, FL
24 December 2024

56491806R00046